OUR PLACES OF WORSHIP

Judaism

Honor Head

WAYLAND

First published in 2009
by Wayland

Copyright © Wayland 2009

Wayland
338 Euston Road
London NW1 3BH

Wayland Australia
Level 17/207 Kent Street
Sydney NSW 2000

Commissioning editor: Jennifer Sanderson
Editor: Jean Coppendale
Designer: Alix Wood
Consultant: Rachel Montagu, teacher of
    Biblical Hebrew and Jewish Studies

British Library Cataloguing in Publication Data
Head, Honor.
    Judaism. – (Our places of worship)
    1. Synagogues – Juvenile literature.
    2. Public worship – Judaism – Juvenile literature.
    3. Judaism – Juvenile literature.
    I. Title II. Series
    296.6'5-dc22

ISBN 978 0 7502 4927 0

This book can be used in conjunction with the interactive CD-Rom, *Our Places of Worship*. To do this, look for ⊙ and the file path. For example, Jewish synagogues can be found on .../Synagogues. From the main menu click on 'Judaism', then 'Synagogues' and then 'Outside a Synagogue' or 'Inside a Synagogue'.

... sample from the CD-Rom, log on to www.waylandbooks.co.uk.

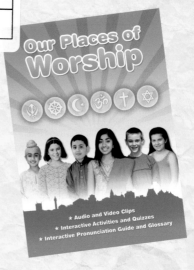

Our Places of Worship

Single user licence: ISBN 978 0 7502 5303 1
School library service licence: ISBN 978 0 7502 5532 5
Site user licence ISBN 978 0 7502 5533 2

Picture credits

Printed in China

Wayland is a division of Hachette Children's Books,
an Hachette UK company.
www.hachette.co.uk

Contents

Words appearing in **bold**, like this, can be found in the glossary on page 30.

What is a synagogue?

A synagogue is where Jews go to worship God and to practise their religion, which is called Judaism. At the synagogue Jews pray, meet other Jewish people and study. From the age of five, Jewish children go to religious classes in the synagogue. Adults may go to classes in the evening. At the classes, both children and adults learn prayers as well as **Hebrew** and Jewish history.

▼ The Singers Hill synagogue in Birmingham, England, was built in 1856.

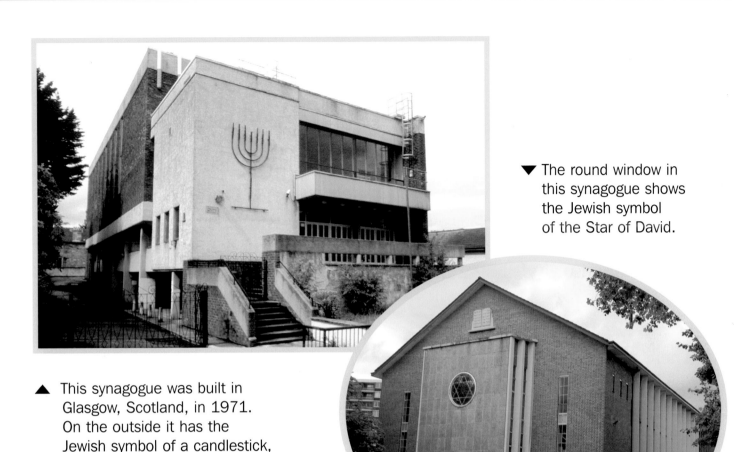

▼ The round window in this synagogue shows the Jewish symbol of the Star of David.

▲ This synagogue was built in Glasgow, Scotland, in 1971. On the outside it has the Jewish symbol of a candlestick, called a **menorah**.

The outside of a synagogue

Synagogues can look very different from each other on the outside. Some synagogues are specially built as a place of worship. Others may have once been used as a school or a house. Many synagogues have Jewish symbols on the outside of the buildings to let people know it is a synagogue. These include the **Star of David** (see page 16) and the menorah (see pages 18-19).

THE HOLY TEMPLE

Thousands of years ago, a Jewish king called Solomon ruled an empire. A place called Israel was the centre of this empire. Solomon built a beautiful temple in Jerusalem, the capital city of Israel. The temple was known as the Holy Temple and was a special building where Jews could worship.

Welcome to the synagogue

Prayers are held at the synagogue every day. However, most people go to the synagogue on Friday evening and Saturday morning to celebrate Shabbat, or the Sabbath. This is a day of rest for Jews all over the world (see pages 12-13). Synagogue services are usually led by a **rabbi**.

Orthodox Jews

There are two main branches, or groups, in Judaism. Orthodox Jews believe in the teachings of God as written in the **Torah** by Moses (see pages 10-11). In Orthodox synagogues, men and women do not sit together. The women and girls sit upstairs in a gallery, or on raised seats behind a screen.

cantor
(see page 20)

rabbi

Ark, or cupboard, where Torah scrolls are kept

women's gallery

raised platform or bimah (see page 8)

▶ Men and women do not sit together in an Orthodox synagogue.

⊙ Judaism/Worship

Reform Jews

Reform Jews believe that the Torah was not written by Moses but by people with guidance from God. They have adapted the laws as a guide to modern life. Reform Jews allow women to become rabbis.

▲ Inside a Reform synagogue, men and women sit together during a service.

▼ Women rabbis often lead the service in a Reform synagogue.

WHAT DO YOU THINK?

Why do you think it matters if men and women sit together during a service?

Why do you think some Jews might not like a woman to become a rabbi?

The holy book

The Torah is the Jewish holy book (see pages 10-11). It is written on scrolls that are kept at the front of the synagogue in a special cupboard called the Ark. Above the Ark is a light called ner tamid, which means 'everlasting light'. This light is never allowed to go out to show that God is always there.

▲ A child is usually asked to undress the Torah scrolls before the service.

Ark where Torah is kept   ner tamid   Torah scrolls   rabbi

Preparing the Torah

During the service, the Torah scrolls are taken out of the Ark. They are often wrapped in velvet covers that are beautifully decorated with Jewish symbols. The scrolls are then unwrapped, or 'undressed'. They are carefully placed on a desk on a raised platform in the middle of the synagogue. This platform is called a bimah.

◀ The Torah is taken out of the Ark by the rabbi before the service begins.

Reading from the Torah

The rabbi reads from the Torah as part of the service. When the reading is finished, the scrolls are taken back to the Ark. The rabbi then gives a sermon, or talk. He may explain part of the Torah or tell a story from it. The rabbi might also talk about an issue that interests Jewish people. The service begins and ends with prayers that are sung from a prayer book called the Siddur.

▲ During the service the rabbi gives a talk. Rabbi means 'my teacher' in Hebrew.

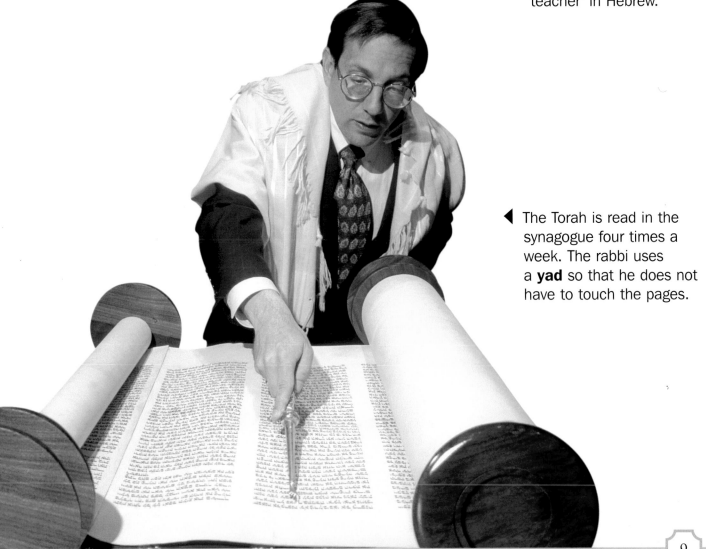

◀ The Torah is read in the synagogue four times a week. The rabbi uses a **yad** so that he does not have to touch the pages.

⊙ Judaism/Worship/Prayer in the Synagogue

The Torah

The Torah is the holiest book for all Jewish people. It is also called the Five Books of Moses. These books contain the early history of the Jews and their laws. Jewish people believe the Torah tells them how God wants them to live and behave. Orthodox Jews believe the Torah is the word of God written down by the **prophet** Moses.

▼ Children can go to special classes in the synagogue, where they are taught how to read and understand the Torah.

⊙ Judaism/Worship

Precious scroll

Each copy of the Torah is very precious and is treated with love and respect. The Torah cover is called a mantle and usually has a silver decoration with bells at the top. Each cover has a silver shield hanging around it and a pointer, or yad. The main Torah reading is done on the Sabbath morning. Readings from the Torah are sung by the rabbi rather than spoken.

▶ The Torah scrolls are wrapped in special decorated covers.

GOD'S COMMANDMENTS

Jews believe that thousands of years ago, Moses led the Jewish people to freedom when they were slaves in Egypt. One night in the desert, at a place called Mount Sinai, God called Moses and gave him ten rules the Jewish people should follow for a good life. These commandments are written down in the Torah.

The yad

Anyone can read the Torah if they speak Hebrew. People use a yad to read the scrolls. Yad means 'hand' and the end of the yad looks like a closed hand with a pointing finger. The yad is used to follow the words. No one must touch the Torah scrolls with their hands as this may damage the scrolls or make them dirty.

Shabbat

On Friday evenings, family and friends gather to celebrate Shabbat, or the Sabbath. Shabbat lasts from sunset on Friday until it is dark on Saturday evening. During this time Jews must not work. Before sunset on Friday, the house is cleaned and all the meals for Shabbat are prepared.

▼ On the Friday evening of Shabbat, a table is laid for a meal. The wife or mother of the family lights two candles to show that Shabbat has begun.

Before the meal on Shabbat, the mother and daughters cover their eyes and say a blessing.

Challah is eaten on Shabbat to remind Jews of the bread God sent their **ancestors** when they escaped from Egypt.

Blessings at home

The wife and daughters say a **blessing** to welcome the day of rest. Then the parents bless the children and everyone wishes each other Shabbat shalom, which means 'peace on the Sabbath'. The family then shares a meal that includes a plaited loaf called challah. Some Jews go to the synagogue for prayers before the meal.

End of Shabbat

At the end of Shabbat, there is a ceremony called havdalah. The family sniffs spices to symbolise carrying the sweetness of Shabbat with them into the rest of the week.

Special clothes

Jewish men and boys wear a skullcap called a kippah when they visit the synagogue. In some synagogues, women and girls also cover their heads with a kippah, a scarf or a hat. Some people wear a prayer shawl called a tallit. The prayer shawl has long fringes that remind Jews of the many laws that are written in the Torah.

▲ A kippah, or skullcap, is worn by Jewish boys and men as a sign of respect for God.

◀ Many men wear a tallit, or prayer shawl, during services in the synagogue or for prayers at home. In a Reform synagogue women can also wear a tallit.

▼ Jewish men wear the tefillin to remind them of the words of God.

WHAT DO YOU THINK?

Why do some people think it is important to cover their head in the synagogue?

What sorts of clothes do you think it would be wrong to wear to a place of worship?

a leather box containing part of the Torah is worn close to the mind

leather straps

a second leather box is worn on the left arm – the arm closest to the heart

The tefillin

Tefillin are sometimes worn by Jewish men when they pray. Tefillin are two small leather boxes with long leather straps. One box is tied to the man's forehead and the other to the upper part of his left arm. Inside the boxes are scrolls of **parchment** with parts of the Torah written on them. They are worn close to the mind and heart during morning prayers.

Signs and symbols

There are many signs and symbols that are very important to Jewish people. The most important symbol is the Magen David, which is also called the Shield of David or the Star of David. It is often used as a decoration in the synagogue and it appears on the flag of Israel. It is called the Star of David because the shape is thought to be the same as the shield of King David, one of the great kings of Israel.

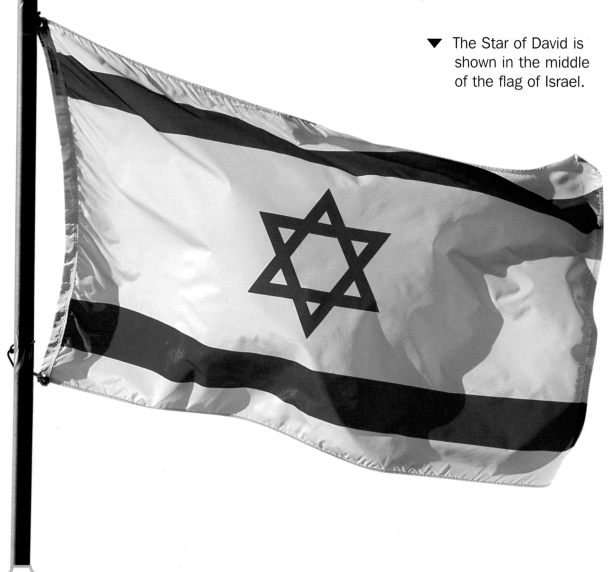

▼ The Star of David is shown in the middle of the flag of Israel.

⊙ Judaism/Signs, Symbols and Religious Objects

The mezuzah

Most Jewish homes have a mezuzah by the front door. This is a small case or box with a prayer inside called the shema. The mezuzah is fixed to the outside part of the door frame to show that it is a Jewish home. Family members touch the mezuzah every time they leave and enter the house. This is a sign that God is always in the home.

▶ The mezuzah is fixed to the right-hand side of the door frame.

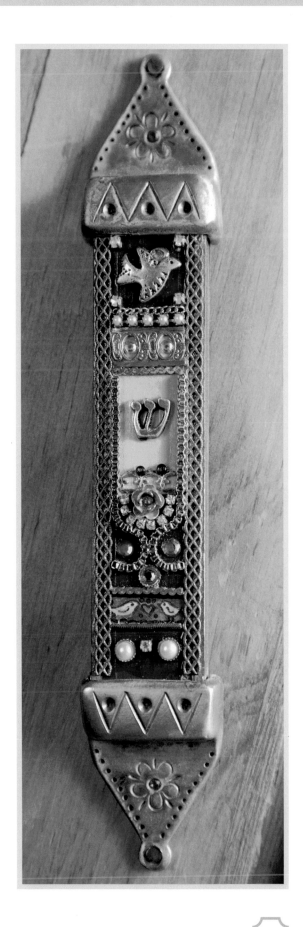

KING DAVID

▲ This statue of King David is in the city of Jerusalem.

For many years the Jews were ruled by kings. One of these was King David. A story in the Torah says that when he was a boy, David killed a giant called Goliath with a stone and a sling. This was to prove that good could overcome evil. King David wrote many of the hymns, called psalms, that are in the Torah.

The menorah

A menorah is a candlestick with seven or nine branches. A menorah with seven branches is used in some synagogues as a reminder of the Holy Temple in Jerusalem. A menorah with nine branches is lit on each day of the festival of Hanukkah.

Hanukkah

Once a year, Jews celebrate Hanukkah, or the Festival of Lights. At this time they remember the time in their history when they fought for the Holy Temple in Jerusalem. They won back the Temple from the enemy but found there was only enough oil in the Temple lamp to last for one day. By a **miracle**, God kept the lamp burning for eight days until more oil arrived.

◀ The menorah decorating this synagogue holds seven candles.

Lighting the candles

The festival of Hanukkah lasts for eight days. During this time Jews use a nine-branch menorah to remind them of the miracle of the burning oil lamp in the Holy Temple. One candle is lit for each night that the lamp burned in the Temple, so one candle is lit on the first day, two on the second and so on, until all the candles are alight. The candle in the middle is used to light the other eight.

▼ A nine-branch menorah is lit during Hanukkah to remember the miracle of the oil lamp in the Holy Temple.

WHAT DO **YOU** THINK?

Why are symbols important to people?

Why you think it is a good idea to use religious symbols as decorations?

Music and musicians

During a service, prayers are sung from the Siddur. These are usually lead by a cantor, or hazzan, who is always a man in an Orthodox synagogue. The cantor has a beautiful voice and he can sing prayers and hymns without any musical backing. The cantor will work with the choir if there is one at the synagogue or he can sing alone. In some Reform synagogues women are also cantors.

▼ In this Reform synagogue, the **congregation** sings hymns together.

◉ Judaism/Worship/Prayer in the Synagogue

▲ This cantor is teaching these twins how to sing the prayers for their Bat and Bar Mitzvah ceremonies.

Hired singers

In some synagogues the cantor may also be the rabbi, or a member of the congregation who is respected and has a knowledge of the prayer service. In larger synagogues, skilled and trained cantors are hired and paid to take part in services.

Teaching others

Cantors also teach members of the congregation how to take part in prayer services and to read from the Torah. They often prepare children for their **Bar** and **Bat Mitzvah** ceremonies (see page 22) and teach adults at the synagogue.

WHAT DO YOU THINK?

Why is music an important part of religious services?

What sort of music do you think would be good for religious services?

Jewish services

Many special Jewish services take place at the synagogue. One of these is the Bar or Bat Mitzvah. Bar Mitzvah is for boys and Bat Mitzvah is for girls. The names mean 'the son or daughter of the commandments'. The Bar Mitzvah service takes place when a boy is 13 years old. At this age, a boy is considered old enough to take on the responsibilities of a man and is allowed to read from the Torah in the synagogue. Girls have a similar ceremony when they become Bat Mitzvah.

▼ These rabbis are teaching this boy how to read the Torah for his Bar Mitzvah.

Wedding day

Most Jewish weddings take place in a synagogue. The bride and groom stand under a canopy called a huppah. This is a symbol of the home they will soon be sharing together, and of God's protection. The rabbi says prayers and blesses the bride and groom who then make their marriage promises, or vows, and exchange wedding rings.

▶ The bride and groom stand under a brightly coloured wedding canopy to say their vows.

WHAT DO **YOU** THINK?

Why do you think a special day to celebrate becoming an adult is important?

What do you think is a good age for a child to become an adult?

Funerals

When a Jewish person dies he or she is buried as soon as possible. A simple service is held in the prayer hall at the **cemetery** and then the body is buried. Jews do not believe in **cremation** because they cannot destroy what God has made. During the service, a special prayer called the kaddish is read.

Holy days

Rosh Hashanah is the Jewish New Year. On the evening before Rosh Hashanah, Jewish families have a special meal together that includes slices of apple dipped in honey. On the day of Rosh Hashanah there is a service in the synagogue. Religious poems are chanted and a special horn called a shofar is blown 100 times.

▲ During Rosh Hashanah, people share apple dipped in honey to wish each other a sweet and a happy new year.

▼ The shofar is made from a ram's horn and is blown to ask God for forgiveness.

Ten Days of Repentance

Rosh Hashanah is the first of ten holy days called the Ten Days of Repentance. This is a time when Jews look back over the past year and say sorry to God for any bad things they have done. They try to make up any quarrels they have had and promise to behave better in the coming year.

Yom Kippur

The tenth day is called Yom Kippur and this is the holiest day of the Jewish year. Jews spend the day in the synagogue praying and asking God for forgiveness. Adults **fast** for 25 hours. At the end of the fast the shofar is blown again to remind people of the promises they have made to God. Children do not fast until they are 12 or 13 years old.

▶ In some synagogues the rabbi wears white robes during Yom Kippur.

Sukkot

Five days after Yom Kippur the festival of Sukkot takes place. As part of the festival, a sukkah is built. A sukkah is a hut made from wood, but the roof is made from leaves or branches so that the sky can be seen. Families build a sukkah in the garden, or one is built near the synagogue where everyone can gather. Jews meet in the sukkah for meals and to remember the time when their ancestors had to live in the desert.

The lulav

During Sukkot, special services are held in the synagogue. Jews wave a lulav, which is made up of branches from willow, palm and myrtle trees. They also hold a citron, a fruit similar to a lemon. The walk around the bimah and wave the lulav in all directions to show that God rules the whole universe.

▶ In the sukkah or synagogue, Jews hold a citron and wave a lulav in all directions.

MEANING OF THE LULAV

Each part of the lulav has a special meaning. The palm is a symbol of the backbone, the myrtle is a symbol of the eyes and the willow is a symbol of the lips. Together, they remind Jews that they must worship God with all their senses and their whole body.

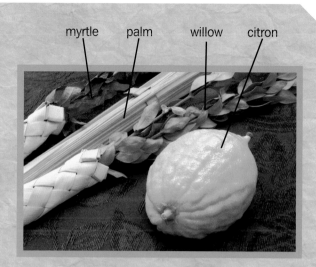

myrtle palm willow citron

▲ The lulav is also made to thank God for a good harvest.

Simchat Torah

The day after Sukkot is Simchat Torah. This is a day to celebrate the Torah. Each week throughout the year, part of the Torah is read out in the synagogue during the service. Simchat Torah is when the very last part of the Torah is read, before starting at the beginning again. Simchat Torah is a very joyful day and children are often given sweets and fruit as part of the celebration.

▲ During Simchat Torah, the Torah scrolls are taken from the Ark and paraded around the synagogue while the people sing and dance.

Holy places

Israel is where the Jewish religion began and this is
where many of the most important holy places for
Jews are. Jerusalem is the capital city of Israel and is
the centre of the Jewish religion and law. Many Jews
make a **pilgrimage** to Jerusalem at least once in their
lives. All synagogues around the world are built so
that they face the city of Jerusalem.

▼ Today, Jerusalem is
divided into the old city
and the new. The old
city is surrounded
by walls.

The Western Wall

In 70 CE, the Roman army destroyed the Holy Temple in Jerusalem. All that remains of the Temple is the Western Wall, which is the most important place of pilgrimage for Jews. As well as saying prayers there, many **pilgrims** and visitors write their prayers on slips of paper and place them in the gaps between the stones of the Wall.

MOUNT SINAI

Mount Sinai is in the Sinai Desert in Egypt. Many pilgrims visit the spot where it is believed God handed the Ten Commandments to Moses.

▼ To Jews, the Western Wall in Jerusalem is the holiest place on Earth. Pilgrims from all over the world go there to pray and to feel closer to God.

Glossary

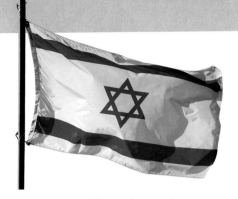

ancestors people from the same family, or group, who lived a long time ago

Bar Mitzvah when a Jewish boy is considered an adult, usually at the age of 13

Bat Mitzvah when a Jewish girl is considered an adult, at the age of 12 or 13

blessing asking God to look after someone or something

cantor a person who is trained to sing in the synagogue

cemetery a place where dead people are buried

congregation a group of people who regularly go to the synagogue to worship

cremation when the body of a dead person is burned instead of buried

fast when someone does not eat or drink for a certain time especially for religious reasons

Hebrew the ancient language of the Jewish people

menorah a candlestick with seven or nine branches used on special occasions. It is also used as a Jewish symbol.

miracle something amazing and wonderful that happens but that cannot be explained

parchment a type of paper

pilgrimage a special journey to a religious place of great importance

pilgrims people who go on special journeys to visit holy places

prophet a messenger from God

rabbi a Jewish teacher and leader

Star of David a star-shaped symbol that is very important to Jewish people

Torah the Jewish holy book. It is made up of the Five Books of Moses and teaches Jews how to live and behave

yad a pointer used for reading the Torah so that the reader does not have to touch the scroll

Quizzes

Try these questions to see how much you remember about Judaism.

Are these facts true or false?

1. Jewish people worship in a synagogue.

2. Challah is a type of bread.

3. Shabbat is celebrated on Thursdays.

4. A menorah is a holy book.

5. A mezuzah is fixed to the door frame.

Match one of these words to each picture.

a. kippah

b. tefillin

c. tallit

Answers are on the next page.

Index

Answers

1 True

2 True

3 False, it is celebrated on Fridays.

4 False, it is a candle holder.

5 True

Match the word to the picture: a3; b2; c1.

OUR PLACES OF WORSHIP

Contents of titles in the series:

Buddhism
978 0 7502 4930 0
What is a temple?
Welcome to the temple
Puja in the temple
Meditation
The Buddha
The Buddha's teachings
Five choices
Signs and symbols
Buddhist festivals
Holy places

Islam
978 0 7502 4925 6
What is a mosque?
Welcome to the mosque
The Imam
What Muslims believe
Muslims at prayer
The Prophet Muhammad (pubh)
The Qu'ran
Signs and symbols
Islamic festivals
Holy places

Christianity
978 0 7502 4926 3
What is a church?
Welcome to the church
A Christian service
Jesus Christ
The Bible
Signs and symbols
Joining the church
Christian festivals
Holy places

Judaism
978 0 7502 4927 0
What is a synagogue?
Welcome to the synagogue
The Torah
Shabbat
Special clothes
Signs and symbols
Music and musicians
Jewish services
Holy days
Holy places

Hinduism
978 0 7502 4929 4
What is a mandir?
Welcome to the mandir
What Hindus believe
Brahman and the deities
Worshipping at home
Holy books
Signs and symbols
Special occasions
Hindu festivals
Holy places

Sikhism
978 0 7502 4928 7
What is a gurdwara?
Welcome to the gurdwara
The Guru Granth Sahib
A Sikh service
Hymns and music
The langar
Signs and symbols
The Gurus
Sikh festivals
Holy places

WAYLAND